Practical
Summer Food

p^3

This is a P³ Book
First published in 2003

P³
Queen Street House
4 Queen Street
Bath BA1 1HE, UK

ISBN: 1-40540-930-4

Printed in China

NOTE

This book uses metric and imperial measurements. Follow the same units
of measurement throughout; do not mix metric and imperial.
All spoon measurements are level: teaspoons are assumed to be 5 ml, and
tablespoons are assumed to be 15 ml. Unless otherwise stated,
milk is assumed to be full fat, eggs and individual vegetables such as potatoes
are medium, and pepper is freshly ground black pepper.

The nutritional information provided for each recipe is per serving or per person.
Optional ingredients, variations, or serving suggestions have not been included
in the calculations. The times given for each recipe are an approximate guide only
because the preparation times may differ according to the techniques used by
different people and the cooking times may vary as a result of the type of oven used.

Recipes using raw or very lightly cooked eggs should be
avoided by children, the elderly, pregnant women, convalescents,
and anyone suffering from an illness.

Contents

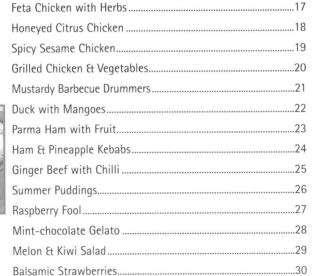

Introduction

Summertime is all about easy living, so when it comes to preparing meals, you want something light on effort yet lively on the taste buds. Fortunately, help and inspiration are to hand with this range of quick and easy, enticing recipes that will bring you the very best of the season. The key to successful summer cooking is to create dishes that capture the essence of the sun-ripened produce readily available in abundance and to let those full-blown flavours and aromas speak for themselves, from the fragrance of herbs, and the heady zest of citrus fruits, to the honeyed-wine scents and tastes of ripe summer berries.

Summer sizzling

Food cooked over hot coals in the balmy outdoors is the quintessential summer eating experience. A barbecue offers the perfect opportunity to relax and have fun with friends and family while enjoying the flavour of summer ingredients at their best, locked in by the heat and intensified by the smoke.

There are many different barbecues to choose from in a variety of sizes, the smaller and lighter being portable or semi-portable. Some have lids that completely cover the barbecue to create oven-like conditions, with the temperature being controlled by vents. Gas and electric barbecues are becoming increasingly popular because they heat up quickly, are easy to regulate, and the lava rock coals are self-cleaning.

Useful accessories

The following accessories will help make barbecuing trouble-free.

Long, insulated gloves or mitts These will protect your hands and forearms from the heat.

Long-handled tongs These are ideal for moving and spreading out briquettes or for positioning and turning foods on the rack. Choose a firm, sturdy pair.

Long-handled basting brush The length of the handle is the important factor here.

Hinged metal racks These come in various shapes and sizes for holding different ingredients such as fish, meat or vegetables, and allow the foods to be turned easily and without the risk of breaking up.

Skewers Metal skewers should be flat to prevent the food slipping around when turning. Wooden skewers need to be soaked for at least 30 minutes before being used so that they do not catch fire.

Water spray gun Keep this handy at all times to douse any flare-ups if necessary, or for dampening down the coals if they are too hot. This is ideal for cleaning the surface of the rack between uses.

Tips for a successful barbecue

Choose a level, sheltered site for setting up the barbecue, well away from vegetation and buildings. If using a charcoal barbecue, always allow enough time for the outside of the coals to burn down to grey ash before cooking – at least 45 minutes, or half an hour for instant-lighting charcoal briquettes.

Brush the rack with vegetable oil, or use a vegetable oil spray, to prevent the foods sticking to it and to aid cleaning. Position the rack about 5 cm/2 inches above the heat. To slow down the cooking, raise the height of the rack; if it is not adjustable, spread out the coals or move food to the edge where the heat will be less intense. Use

the outer portion of the barbecue for cooking thicker pieces of food.

When cooking kebabs, brush metal skewers with oil before using. Choose a combination of ingredients that will cook at the same rate and in the same time and leave a small, even amount of space in between; do not pack them tightly or they may not cook through properly.

Vegetables and other foods can be wrapped in foil with seasonings and a little stock or wine, and cooked on the barbecue to enclose all their juices and leave them tender. Be sure to use heavy-duty aluminium foil for this purpose.

Choose only good-quality, lean cuts of meat for barbecuing to ensure tenderness. Trim most of the fat from around steaks or chops to prevent flare-ups but leave a little to lubricate the meat.

Hardwood chips, such as hickory, or fruitwood chips, such as apple or cherry, contribute an extra smoky quality to barbecued foods. Soak the chips for about an hour (longer if using chunks) before sprinkling over the hot coals, to prevent them burning.

Alfresco food

Picnics are another wonderful way of enjoying summer food in whatever environment takes your fancy, from the beach or woods to your own garden.

To keep foods cool in high temperatures, transport them in a cooler bag. A full cooler bag will keep foods colder than one that it is partially filled, but the latter can be topped up with extra ice packs or large chunks of ice – these stay frozen longer than smaller ice cubes. Position the cooler in the shade. Keep chilled soups, or fruit salads, ice-cold by storing them in wide-necked vacuum flasks.

To serve foods warm, put them into airtight containers, wrap tightly in heavy-duty aluminium foil, then wrap again in several sheets of newspaper.

To keep salads crisp, do not add the dressing until you are ready to serve. Transport the dressing in a screw-top jar and simply shake before pouring over the salad.

Make desserts in individual servings, rather than as one dish, as these are less space-consuming and much easier to serve at the picnic site.

Summer celebrations

There is no need to labour over preparing and cooking elaborate dishes for a celebratory meal. With a few stylish presentation ideas, you can elevate simple summer classics into studies in elegant sophistication.

Herb leaves and flowers and other edible summer flowers, such as mint leaves, chive flowers, rose petals or buds, jasmine flowers, pansies and nasturtiums, can be used decoratively and for an additional touch of fragrant flavour. Wash thoroughly and scatter over salads or use to decorate fruit salads and other desserts. Herbs such as

parsley and tarragon can be finely chopped and beaten into softened butter, then rolled out and shapes stamped out with fancy cutters, to garnish meat and fish dishes. Pretty blue borage flowers, which have a distinctive cucumber-like flavour, or other herb flowers and leaves, can be added to half-filled ice-cube trays, topped up with water and then frozen, to add to punches and other chilled drinks. Or why not make a whole ice bowl by adding herb flowers to the gap between a small and medium-sized freezerproof glass bowl placed one inside the other and taped into position, filled up with water and then frozen? This is ideal for presenting sorbets and ice creams or fruit salads.

Rice salads, or a rice accompaniment, can also be imaginatively presented, pressed into individual fluted moulds or one large ring mould, and upturned on to individual plates or a serving platter to make an attractive centrepiece.

KEY	
	Simplicity level 1–3 (1 easiest, 3 slightly harder)
	Preparation time
	Cooking time

Garlic & Almond Soup

This pretty, pale, chilled soup looks beautiful with its unusual garnish of sliced white grapes and a swirl of olive oil.

30 mins, plus chilling   0 mins

SERVES 4–6

INGREDIENTS

400 g/14 oz day-old French bread, sliced

4 large garlic cloves

1 litre/1¾ pints water, chilled

3–4 tbsp sherry vinegar

6 tbsp extra-virgin olive oil

225 g/8 oz ground almonds

sea salt and pepper

TO GARNISH

seedless white grapes, chilled and sliced

pepper

extra-virgin olive oil

1 Tear the bread into small pieces and put in a bowl. Pour over enough cold water to cover, and soak for 10–15 minutes. Using your hands, squeeze the bread dry. Transfer the moist bread to a food processor.

COOK'S TIP

Instead of grapes, serve with Garlic Croûtons and diced vegetables (see the Gazpacho recipe opposite). Alternatively, sprinkle with a dusting of paprika or very finely chopped fresh parsley just before serving.

2 Cut the garlic cloves in half lengthways and use the tip of the knife to remove the pale green or white cores. Add to the food processor with 3 tablespoons of the sherry vinegar and 225 ml/8 fl oz of the water, and process until blended. Add the oil and ground almonds and blend again.

3 With the motor running, slowly pour in the remaining water until a smooth

soup forms. Add extra sherry vinegar to taste, and season with salt and pepper. Transfer the soup to a bowl, cover, and chill in the refrigerator for at least 4 hours.

4 To serve, adjust the seasoning. Ladle into bowls and float grapes on top. Garnish each with a sprinkling of pepper and a swirl of olive oil. Serve while still very cold.

Iced Gazpacho

This delicious soup, with its brightly coloured garnish of peppers, cucumber and spring onions, is perfect to serve at a summer party.

NUTRITIONAL INFORMATION

Calories	164	Sugars	.........7g
Protein	.........3g	Fat	..........12g
Carbohydrate	...13g	Saturates	.......3g

20 mins, plus chilling
5 mins

SERVES 4–6

I N G R E D I E N T S

2 ripe red peppers

1 cucumber

450 g/1 lb large, juicy tomatoes, skinned, deseeded and coarsely chopped

4 tbsp olive oil

2 tbsp sherry vinegar

salt and pepper

GARLIC CROUTONS

2 tbsp olive oil

1 garlic clove, halved

2 slices bread, crusts removed, cut into 5-mm/¼-inch cubes

sea salt

TO GARNISH

green pepper, diced

red pepper, diced

cucumber, deseeded and finely diced

spring onions, chopped

ice cubes

sprigs of fresh parsley, or other herbs

1 Cut the red peppers in half and remove the cores and seeds, then chop coarsely. Peel the cucumber, cut it in half lengthways, then cut into quarters. Remove the seeds with a teaspoon, then chop the flesh coarsely.

2 Put the red peppers, cucumber and tomatoes in a food processor with the olive oil and sherry vinegar and then process until smooth. Season the soup with salt and pepper to taste. Transfer to a bowl, cover with clingfilm, and chill for at least 4 hours.

3 Meanwhile, to make the croûtons, heat the oil in a frying pan over a medium-high heat. Add the garlic and sauté, stirring, for 2 minutes to flavour the oil.

4 Lift out and discard the garlic. Add the bread cubes and cook until golden on all sides. Drain well on crumpled kitchen paper and sprinkle with sea salt. Store in an airtight container if not using at once.

5 To serve, place each of the vegetable garnishes in bowls for guests to add to their soup. Taste the soup and adjust the seasoning if necessary. Put ice cubes into soup bowls, then ladle over the soup. Top with sprigs of parsley and serve at once.

Pan Bagna

This French sandwich is a cornucopia of the best Mediterranean flavours and never follows a set recipe. Treat this version as a suggestion.

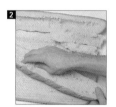
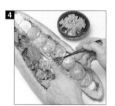
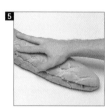

NUTRITIONAL INFORMATION

Calories	422	Sugars	4g
Protein	27g	Fat	16g
Carbohydrate	44g	Saturates	3g

15 mins, plus chilling • 0 mins

SERVES 4

INGREDIENTS

40-cm/16-inch long loaf of country bread, thicker than a French baguette

about 2 tbsp fruity extra-virgin olive oil

black or green olive tapenade, for spreading (optional)

FILLING

2 eggs, hard-boiled and shelled

50 g/1¾ oz anchovy fillets in oil

85 g/3 oz flavoured olives of your choice

lettuce or rocket leaves, rinsed and patted dry

about 4 plum tomatoes, sliced

200 g/7 oz canned tuna in brine, well drained and flaked

1 Slice the eggs. Drain the anchovies, then cut them in half lengthways. Stone the olives and slice in half.

2 Slice the loaf in half lengthways. Pull out about 1 cm/½ inch of the crumb from the centre of each half, leaving a border all around both halves.

3 Generously brush both halves with olive oil. Spread with tapenade, if you like a strong flavour. Arrange lettuce or rocket leaves on the bottom half.

4 Add layers of hard-boiled egg slices, tomato slices, olive halves, drained anchovies and tuna, sprinkling with olive oil and adding lettuce or rocket leaves between the layers. Make the filling as thick as you like.

5 Place the other bread half on top and press down firmly. Wrap tightly in clingfilm and place on a board or plate that will fit in your refrigerator. Weigh it down and chill for several hours. To serve, slice the into 4 equal portions, tying with string to secure in place, if desired.

VARIATION

Other typical Mediterranean fillings for a Pan Bagna include crushed garlic, red or green peppers, young broad beans, gherkins, artichoke hearts, Spanish onions, fresh herbs, and stoned olives.

Greek Strained Yogurt

This smooth and creamy yogurt makes a refreshing start to hot days.
The nutritional information refers to each tablespoon of yogurt.

NUTRITIONAL INFORMATION

Calories 32	Sugars 3g
Protein 2g	Fat 1g
Carbohydrate 3g	Saturates 1g

 36½ hrs   0 mins

MAKES 500 ML/18 FL OZ

I N G R E D I E N T S

1 litre/1¾ pints natural yogurt

½ tsp salt

O P T I O N A L   T O P P I N G S

fruity extra-virgin olive oil

orange blossom honey or lavender honey

coriander seeds, crushed

paprika

very finely chopped fresh mint or coriander

finely grated lemon rind

1 Place a 125 x 75-cm/50 x 30-inch piece of muslin in a saucepan, cover with water, and bring to the boil. Remove the pan from the heat and, using a wooden spoon, lift out the muslin. Wearing rubber gloves to protect your hands, wring the muslin dry.

2 Fold the muslin into a double layer and use it to line a colander or sieve set over a large bowl. Put the yogurt in a bowl and stir in the salt, then spoon into the centre of the muslin.

3 Tie the muslin so it is suspended above the bowl. If your sink is deep enough, gather up the corners of the muslin and tie it to the tap. If not, lay a broom handle across 2 chairs and put the bowl between the chairs. Tie the muslin to the broom handle. Remove the colander or sieve and let the yogurt drain into the bowl for at least 12 hours.

4 Transfer the yogurt to a nylon sieve placed in a bowl. Cover lightly with clingfilm and refrigerate for 24 hours until soft and creamy. The yogurt will keep in the refrigerator for up to 5 days.

5 To serve, taste and add extra salt if needed. Spoon the yogurt into a bowl and sprinkle with the topping of your choice or a combination of toppings.

Caesar Salad

This salad was the invention of a chef at Caesar's, a restaurant in Tijuana, Mexico. It has rightly earned an international reputation.

NUTRITIONAL INFORMATION

Calories 589	Sugars 3g	
Protein 11g	Fat 50g	
Carbohydrate ...24g	Saturates 9g	

25 mins   15–20 mins

SERVES 4

INGREDIENTS

1 large cos lettuce, or 2 Little Gem lettuces

4 canned anchovies in oil, drained and halved lengthways

Parmesan shavings, to garnish

DRESSING

2 garlic cloves, crushed

1½ tsp Dijon mustard

1 tsp Worcestershire sauce

4 canned anchovies in olive oil, drained and chopped

1 egg yolk

1 tbsp lemon juice

150 ml/5 fl oz olive oil

4 tbsp freshly grated Parmesan cheese

salt and pepper

CROUTONS

4 thick slices day-old bread

2 tbsp olive oil

1 garlic clove, crushed

1 First, make the dressing. Put the garlic, mustard, Worcestershire sauce, anchovies, egg yolk, lemon juice, and seasoning into a food processor or blender and process for 30 seconds until foaming. Add the oil, drop by drop, until the mixture begins to thicken, then in a steady stream until all the oil is incorporated. Scrape out of the food processor or blender. Add a little hot water if the dressing is too thick. Stir in the grated Parmesan cheese. Taste for seasoning and set aside in the refrigerator until required.

2 For the croûtons, cut the bread into 1-cm/½-inch cubes. Toss with the olive oil and garlic in a bowl. Spread out on a baking sheet in a single layer. Bake in a preheated oven, 180°C/350°F/Gas Mark 4, for 15–20 minutes, stirring occasionally, until the croûtons are browned and crisp. Remove from the oven and set aside to cool.

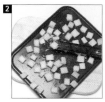

3 Separate the lettuce into individual leaves and wash and spin dry in a salad spinner or pat dry on kitchen paper (excess moisture will dilute the dressing). Transfer to a plastic bag and place in the refrigerator until needed.

4 To assemble the salad, tear the lettuce into pieces and place in a large serving bowl. Add the dressing and toss well. Top with the halved anchovies and the croûtons and Parmesan shavings. Serve immediately.

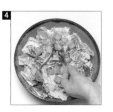

Tuna Niçoise Salad

This is a classic version of the French salade niçoise. It is a substantial salad, suitable for a lunch or light summer supper.

NUTRITIONAL INFORMATION

Calories 109	Sugars 1g	
Protein 7g	Fat 7g	
Carbohydrate 5g	Saturates 1g	

  10 mins   20 mins

SERVES 4

I N G R E D I E N T S

4 eggs

450 g/1 lb new potatoes

115 g/4 oz small French beans, trimmed and halved

2 tuna steaks, about 175 g/6 oz each

1–2 tbsp olive oil, for brushing

2 Little Gem lettuces

200 g/7 oz cherry tomatoes, halved

175 g/6 oz cucumber, peeled, cut in half, and sliced

55 g/2 oz stoned black olives

55 g/2 oz canned anchovies in olive oil, drained

D R E S S I N G

1 garlic clove, crushed

1½ tsp Dijon mustard

2 tsp lemon juice

2 tbsp chopped fresh basil

5 tbsp olive oil

salt and pepper

1 Bring a small saucepan of water to the boil. Add the eggs and then cook for 7–9 minutes from when the water returns to the boil – 7 minutes for a slightly soft centre or 9 minutes for a firm centre. Drain and refresh under cold running water. Set aside.

2 Cook the potatoes in lightly salted boiling water for 10–12 minutes until tender. Add the beans 3 minutes before the end of the cooking time. Drain both vegetables well and refresh under cold water. Drain well again.

3 Wash and dry the tuna steaks. Brush with a little olive oil and season to taste. Cook on a preheated ridged grill pan for 2–3 minutes each side until just tender but still slightly pink in the centre. Set aside to rest.

4 To make the dressing, whisk together the garlic, mustard, lemon juice, basil, olive oil and seasoning.

5 To assemble the salad, break apart the lettuces and tear into large pieces. Divide among individual serving plates. Next, add the potatoes and beans, with the tomatoes, cucumber and olives. Toss lightly together. Shell the eggs and cut into quarters lengthways. Arrange these on top of the salad. Scatter the anchovies over the top.

6 Flake the tuna steaks and arrange on the salad. Pour over the dressing and serve.

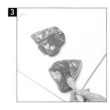

Orange & Fennel Salad

Fresh, juicy oranges and the sharp aniseed flavour of fennel combine to make this refreshing Spanish salad.

NUTRITIONAL INFORMATION

Calories ......136 Sugars 19g
Protein ....3g Fat 6g
Carbohydrate ...19g Saturates 1g

30 mins   0 mins

SERVES 4

INGREDIENTS

4 large oranges

1 large bulb of fennel

2 tsp fennel seeds

2 tbsp extra-virgin olive oil

freshly squeezed orange juice, to taste

fresh parsley, finely chopped, to garnish

1 Using a small serrated knife, remove the rind and pith from 1 orange, cutting carefully from the top to the bottom of the orange so that it retains its shape. Work over a small bowl to catch the juices.

2 Peel the remaining oranges the same way, reserving all the juices. Cut the oranges horizontally into 5-mm/¼-inch slices and arrange in an attractive serving bowl; reserve the juices.

VARIATION

Replace the fennel with a finely sliced onion or a large bunch of spring onions, finely chopped. This version is from Spain, where orange-coloured oranges would be used, but in Sicily the dish is made with blood-red oranges.

3 Cut the fronds from the fennel bulb, cut the bulb in half lengthways, and then into quarters. Cut crossways into very thin slices. Immediately place in the bowl of oranges and toss with a little of the reserved juice to prevent discolouration.

4 Sprinkle the fennel seeds over the oranges and sliced fennel.

5 Whisk the olive oil with the remaining reserved orange juice, plus extra fresh orange juice to taste. Pour over the oranges and fennel and toss gently. Cover with clingfilm and chill until ready to serve.

6 Just before serving, remove from the refrigerator and sprinkle with parsley. Serve chilled.

Tofu Skewers

Although tofu is rather bland on its own, it develops
a fabulous flavour when it is marinated in garlic and herbs.

Calories	149	Sugars	.........5g
Protein	........13g	Fat	...........9g
Carbohydrate	....5g	Saturates	......1g

40 mins   15 mins

SERVES 4

INGREDIENTS

350 g/12 oz tofu

1 red pepper

1 yellow pepper

2 courgettes

8 white mushrooms

lemon slices, to garnish

MARINADE

grated rind and juice of ½ lemon

1 garlic clove, crushed

½ tsp chopped fresh rosemary

½ tsp chopped fresh thyme

1 tbsp walnut oil

1 To make the marinade, mix the lemon rind and juice, garlic, rosemary, thyme and oil in a shallow, non-metallic dish.

2 Drain the tofu, pat it dry on kitchen paper and cut it into squares with a sharp knife. Add to the marinade and toss to coat. Cover and set aside to marinate for 20–30 minutes.

3 Meanwhile, deseed and cut the peppers into 2.5-cm/1-inch pieces. Blanch in boiling water for 4 minutes, refresh in cold water and drain.

4 Using a canelle knife or potato peeler, remove strips of peel from the courgettes. Cut the courgettes into 2.5-cm/ 1-inch chunks.

5 Remove the tofu from the marinade, reserving the liquid. Thread it onto 8 skewers, alternating with the peppers, courgettes and mushrooms.

6 Cook the skewers over medium hot coals for about 6 minutes, turning and basting with the reserved marinade. Alternatively, cook under a preheated grill. Transfer the skewers to warmed individual serving plates, garnish with slices of lemon and serve.

Poached Rainbow Trout

This colourful, flavoursome dish can be served cold and therefore makes a lovely summer lunch or alfresco supper dish.

NUTRITIONAL INFORMATION

Calories 99	Sugars 1g
Protein 6g	Fat 6g
Carbohydrate 4g	Saturates 1g

🍖 🍖 🍖

🧊 25 mins   🕐 1 hr

SERVES 4

I N G R E D I E N T S

1.3 kg/3 lb rainbow trout fillets

700 g/1 lb 9 oz new potatoes

3 spring onions, finely chopped

1 egg, hard-boiled and chopped

fresh salad leaves, to serve

C O U R T - B O U I L L O N

850 ml/1½ pints cold water

850 ml/1½ pints dry white wine

3 tbsp white wine vinegar

2 large carrots, coarsely chopped

1 onion, coarsely chopped

2 celery sticks, coarsely chopped

2 leeks, coarsely chopped

2 garlic cloves, coarsely chopped

2 fresh bay leaves

4 sprigs each fresh parsley and thyme

6 black peppercorns

1 tsp salt

M A Y O N N A I S E

1 egg yolk

1 tsp Dijon mustard

1 tsp white wine vinegar

55 g/2 oz watercress or baby spinach leaves, chopped

225 ml/8 fl oz light olive oil

salt and pepper

1 First make the court-bouillon. Place all the ingredients in a large saucepan and bring to the boil over a low heat. Cover and simmer for about 30 minutes. Strain the liquid through a fine sieve into a clean saucepan. Bring to the boil again and then simmer rapidly, uncovered, for 15–20 minutes until the court-bouillon is reduced to about 600 ml/1 pint.

2 Put the trout in a large frying pan. Add the court-bouillon and bring to the boil over a low heat. Remove from the heat and set the fish aside in the liquid to cool.

3 Meanwhile, make the mayonnaise. Put the egg yolk, Dijon mustard, white wine vinegar, watercress or spinach, and salt and pepper to taste into a food processor or blender and process for 30 seconds until foaming. Begin adding the olive oil, drop by drop, until the mixture begins to thicken. Continue adding the oil in a slow, steady stream until it is all incorporated. Add a little hot water if the mixture seems too thick. Season to taste and set aside.

4 Cook the potatoes in plenty of lightly salted boiling water for about 12–15 minutes until soft and tender. Drain well and refresh them under cold running water. Set the potatoes aside until cold.

5 When the potatoes are cold, cut them in half, if they are very large, and toss thoroughly with the mayonnaise, finely chopped spring onions and hard-boiled egg.

6 Carefully lift the fish from the poaching liquid and drain on kitchen paper. Carefully pull the skin away from each of the trout fillets. Serve immediately with the potato salad and salad leaves, or leave to cool and serve chilled.

Red Mullet & Coconut Loaf

This fish and coconut loaf is ideal to take along on picnics because it can be served cold as well as hot.

 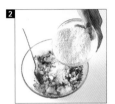 

NUTRITIONAL INFORMATION

Calories	138	Sugars	........12g
Protein	.........11g	Fat	...........1g
Carbohydrate	...23g	Saturates	......0g

  15 mins 🕐 1¼ hrs

SERVES 4–6

INGREDIENTS

225 g/8 oz red mullet fillets, skinned

2 tomatoes, deseeded and finely chopped

2 green peppers, finely chopped

1 onion, finely chopped

1 fresh red chilli, finely chopped

150 g/5½ oz breadcrumbs

600 ml/1 pint coconut liquid (see step 2, below)

salt and pepper

HOT PEPPER SAUCE

125 ml/4 fl oz tomato ketchup

1 tsp West Indian hot pepper sauce

¼ tsp hot mustard

TO GARNISH

twists of fresh lemon

sprigs of fresh chervil

1 Finely chop the fish and mix with the tomatoes, green peppers, onion and fresh chilli.

2 Stir in the breadcrumbs, coconut liquid and seasoning. If using fresh coconut, use a hammer and the tip of a sturdy knife to poke out the 'eyes' in the top and pour out the liquid.

3 Grease a 500-g/1 lb 2-oz loaf tin and line the base. Add the fish mixture.

4 Bake in a preheated oven, 200°C/400°F/Gas Mark 6, for 1–1¼ hours until set.

5 To make the hot pepper sauce, combine the tomato ketchup, West Indian hot pepper sauce, and mustard until smooth and creamy.

6 Cut the loaf into slices, garnish with lemon twists and chervil, and serve hot or cold with the sauce.

COOK'S TIP

Be careful when preparing chillies because the juices can irritate the skin, especially the face. Wash your hands after handling them or wear clean rubber gloves to prepare them if preferred.

Barbecued Monkfish

Monkfish cooks very well on a barbecue because it is a firm-fleshed fish. Make sure that you remove the membrane before cooking.

NUTRITIONAL INFORMATION

Calories 219   Sugars 0g
Protein . . . . .28g   Fat 12g
Carbohydrate . . . .1g   Saturates 2g

 2¼ hrs   5–6 mins

SERVES 4

INGREDIENTS

700 g/1 lb 9 oz monkfish fillet, cut into chunks

2 limes, each cut into 6 wedges

sprigs of fresh basil, to garnish

freshly cooked noodles, to serve

MARINADE

4 tbsp olive oil

grated rind of 1 lime

2 tsp Thai fish sauce

2 garlic cloves, crushed

1 tsp grated fresh root ginger

2 tbsp chopped fresh basil

salt and pepper

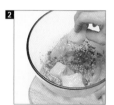  

1 To make the marinade, combine the olive oil, lime rind, fish sauce, garlic, grated ginger, and basil in a non-metallic bowl. Season to taste and set aside.

VARIATION

You could use any type of white-fleshed fish for this recipe but sprinkle the pieces with salt and leave for 2 hours to firm the flesh, before rinsing, drying, and then adding to the marinade.

2 Wash the monkfish chunks and then pat them dry with kitchen paper. Add them to the marinade and mix well to coat. Cover the bowl and set aside in the refrigerator to marinate for 2 hours, stirring occasionally.

3 If you are using bamboo skewers, soak them in cold water for 30 minutes to prevent them charring.

4 Lift the monkfish pieces from the marinade with a slotted spoon and thread them on to the skewers, alternating with the lime wedges.

5 Transfer the skewers, either to a hot barbecue or to a preheated ridged grill pan. Cook for 5–6 minutes, turning regularly, until the fish is tender. Garnish with sprigs of basil and serve with noodles.

Feta Chicken with Herbs

Chicken goes well with most savoury herbs, especially during the summer when fresh herbs are at their best.

NUTRITIONAL INFORMATION

Calories ...... .283 Sugars 5g
Protein .... .25g Fat .... .15g
Carbohydrate ...14g Saturates 2g

🗓 15–20 mins   🕐 25–30 mins

SERVES 4

I N G R E D I E N T S

8 skinless, boneless chicken thighs

2 tbsp each chopped fresh thyme, rosemary and oregano

125 g/4½ oz feta cheese

1 tbsp milk

2 tbsp plain flour

salt and pepper

thyme, rosemary and oregano, to garnish

freshly cooked green vegetables, to serve

T O M A T O S A U C E

1 medium onion, coarsely chopped

1 garlic clove, crushed

1 tbsp olive oil

4 medium plum tomatoes, cut into quarters

sprig each of thyme, rosemary and oregano

1 Spread out the chicken thighs, smooth side downwards.

2 Divide the herbs among the chicken thighs, then cut the cheese into eight sticks. Place one stick of cheese in the centre of each chicken thigh. Season well, then roll up the thighs to enclose the cheese.

3 Place the chicken thighs in an ovenproof dish, brush them with milk, and dust with flour to coat.

4 Bake in a preheated oven, 190°C/ 375°F/Gas Mark 5, for 25–30 minutes or until golden brown. The juices should run clear and not pink when the chicken is pierced with a skewer in the thickest part.

5 Meanwhile, to make the sauce, cook the onion and garlic in the oil, stirring, until softened and starting to brown.

6 Add the tomatoes, lower the heat, cover, and simmer for 15–20 minutes or until soft.

7 Add the herbs, then blend to a paste in a food processor. Press through a sieve to make a smooth, rich sauce. Season and serve the sauce with the chicken and green vegetables, garnished with herbs.

Honeyed Citrus Chicken

This low-fat recipe is great for summer entertaining. If you cut the chicken in half and press it flat you can roast it in under an hour.

NUTRITIONAL INFORMATION

Calories 288   Sugars 32g
Protein . . . . .30g   Fat 6g
Carbohydrate . . .32g   Saturates 1g

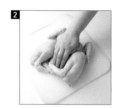

 15–20 mins, plus chilling   45–50 mins

SERVES 4

INGREDIENTS

2 kg/4 lb 8 oz chicken

2 oranges, cut into wedges

salt and pepper

sprigs of fresh tarragon, to garnish

MARINADE

300 ml/10 fl oz orange juice

3 tbsp cider vinegar

3 tbsp honey

2 tbsp chopped fresh tarragon

SAUCE

handful of tarragon sprigs, chopped

200 g/7 oz fat-free fromage frais

2 tbsp orange juice

1 tsp honey

60 g/2¼ oz stuffed olives, chopped

1 Put the chicken on a chopping board with the breast downwards. Cut through the bottom part of the carcass using poultry shears or heavy kitchen scissors, making sure not to cut right through to the breastbone below.

2 Rinse the chicken with cold water, drain, and place on a board with the skin side uppermost. Press the chicken flat, then cut off the leg ends.

3 Thread two long wooden skewers through the bird to keep it flat. Season the skin.

4 Mix all the marinade ingredients in a shallow, non-metallic dish. Add the chicken. Cover and chill for 4 hours, turning the chicken several times.

5 To make the sauce, mix all the ingredients and season. Spoon into a serving dish, cover and chill.

6 Transfer the chicken and marinade to a roasting tin, open out the chicken, and place skin-side downwards. Tuck the orange wedges around the chicken and roast in a preheated oven, 200°C/400°F/Gas Mark 6, for 25 minutes. Remove from the oven and turn the chicken over, return to the oven and roast for another 20–30 minutes. Baste until the chicken is browned and the juices run clear when pierced with a skewer. Garnish the chicken with tarragon and serve with the sauce.

Spicy Sesame Chicken

This is a quick and easy recipe for the grill or barbecue, perfect for lunch or to eat outdoors on a picnic.

NUTRITIONAL INFORMATION

Calories	110	Sugars	.........3g
Protein	........15g	Fat	...........4g
Carbohydrate	....3g	Saturates	......1g

🥔 5 mins   🕐 15 mins

SERVES 4

I N G R E D I E N T S

4 chicken quarters

150 ml/5 fl oz low-fat natural yogurt

finely grated rind and juice of 1 small lemon

2 tsp medium-hot curry paste

1 tbsp sesame seeds

T O   S E R V E

fresh salad

naan bread

wedges of fresh lemon

1 Remove the skin from the chicken and slash the flesh at intervals with a sharp knife.

2 Combine the yogurt, lemon rind and lemon juice and curry paste in a bowl.

3 Spread the mixture over the chicken and arrange on a foil-lined grill rack or baking sheet.

4 Place on a barbecue or under a preheated grill and cook, turning once, for 12–15 minutes until golden and cooked. Test by piercing the thickest part with a skewer; the juices should run clear. Just before the end of the cooking time, sprinkle with the sesame seeds.

5 Serve with a fresh salad, naan bread, and lemon wedges.

VARIATION

Poppy seeds, fennel seeds or cumin seeds, or a mixture of all three, can also be used to sprinkle over the chicken.

Grilled Chicken & Vegetables

Grilling is a quick, healthy cooking method, ideal for sealing in the juices of chicken breasts, and a wonderful way to cook summer vegetables.

NUTRITIONAL INFORMATION

Calories	611	Sugars	........11g
Protein	........43g	Fat	..........21g
Carbohydrate	...66g	Saturates	.......3g

15 mins, plus draining/ marinating

25 mins

SERVES 4

INGREDIENTS

1 small aubergine, sliced

4 boneless chicken breasts

2 medium courgettes, sliced

1 medium red pepper, cut into quarters

1 small bulb of fennel, thickly sliced

1 large red onion, thickly sliced

1 small ciabatta loaf or 1 French baguette, sliced

MARINADE

2 garlic cloves, crushed

finely grated zest of ½ lemon

1 tbsp chopped fresh mint

6 tbsp olive oil, plus extra for brushing/drizzling

salt and pepper

1 Place the aubergine in a colander and sprinkle with salt. Stand over a bowl to drain for 30 minutes, then rinse and dry. This will draw out the bitter juices.

2 To make the marinade, mix together the garlic, lemon zest, mint, olive oil and seasoning.

3 Slash the chicken breasts at intervals with a sharp knife. Spoon over about half of the marinade and stir to combine.

4 Combine the aubergine slices and the remaining vegetables, then toss them in the remaining marinade. Let the chicken and vegetables marinate for about 30 minutes.

5 Cook the chicken and vegetables under a preheated hot grill or on a barbecue for about 20 minutes, turning them occasionally to prevent them burning and sticking, until they are golden brown and tender. Alternatively, cook them in a ridged grill pan on the hob.

6 Brush the bread slices with olive oil and grill or barbecue until golden.

7 Drizzle a little olive oil over the chicken and vegetables and serve hot or cold with the toasted bread.

Mustardy Barbecue Drummers

This is an easy and tasty recipe for chicken drumsticks and is great for barbecues or simple summer lunches and picnics.

NUTRITIONAL INFORMATION

Calories	394	Sugars	.........5g
Protein	........40g	Fat	..........27g
Carbohydrate	....3g	Saturates	......8g

 10–15 mins 25 mins

SERVES 4

I N G R E D I E N T S

10 rashers smoked streaky bacon

1 garlic clove, peeled and finely chopped

3 tbsp whole-grain mustard

4 tbsp fresh brown breadcrumbs

8 chicken drumsticks

1 tbsp sunflower oil

sprigs of fresh parsley, to garnish

1 Chop two of the bacon rashers into small pieces and dry cook in a frying pan for 3–4 minutes, stirring so that the bacon does not stick to the bottom. Remove from the heat and stir in the garlic, 2 tablespoons of the wholegrain mustard, and the breadcrumbs.

2 Using your fingers, carefully loosen the skin from each drumstick, taking care not to tear the skin. Spoon a little of the mustard stuffing under each flap of skin, smoothing the skins over firmly after you have inserted the stuffing.

3 Wrap a bacon rasher around each drumstick; secure with cocktail sticks.

4 Mix together the remaining mustard and the oil and brush over the chicken drumsticks. Cook on a preheated moderately hot barbecue or under a preheated medium-hot grill for about 25 minutes until there is no trace of pink in the juices when the thickest part of the chicken is pierced with a skewer.

5 Garnish with sprigs of fresh parsley and serve hot or cold.

COOK'S TIP

Do not cook the chicken over the hottest part of the barbecue or the outside may be charred before the centre is cooked.

Duck with Mangoes

Use fresh mangoes in this recipe for a terrific flavour and colour. If they are unavailable, use canned mangoes and rinse them before using.

NUTRITIONAL INFORMATION	
Calories 235	Sugars 6g
Protein 23g	Fat 14g
Carbohydrate 6g	Saturates 2g

🌶 🌶 🌶

🥘 5 mins   🕐 35 mins

SERVES 4

I N G R E D I E N T S

2 ripe mangoes

300 ml/10 fl oz chicken stock

2 garlic cloves, crushed

1 tsp grated fresh root ginger

2 large, skinless duck breasts,
    about 225 g/8 oz each

3 tbsp vegetable oil

1 tsp wine vinegar

1 tsp light soy sauce

1 leek, sliced

chopped fresh parsley, to garnish

1 Peel the mangoes and cut the flesh from each side of the stones. Cut the flesh into strips.

2 Put half of the mango pieces and all the chicken stock in a food processor and process until smooth. Alternatively, press half of the mangoes through a fine sieve and mix with the stock.

3 Rub the garlic and ginger over the duck breasts. Heat the oil in a preheated wok and cook the duck breasts, turning frequently, until sealed. Reserve the oil in the wok and remove the duck.

4 Place the duck breasts on a rack set over a roasting tin and cook in a preheated oven, 220°C/425°F/Gas Mark 7, for about 20 minutes until the duck is cooked through and tender.

5 Meanwhile, place the mango and stock mixture in a saucepan and add the wine vinegar and light soy sauce.

6 Bring the mixture to the boil and cook over a high heat, stirring constantly, until reduced by half.

7 Heat the oil reserved in the wok and stir-fry the sliced leek and remaining mango for 1 minute. Remove from the wok, transfer to a serving dish, and keep warm until required.

8 Slice the cooked duck breasts and arrange the slices on top of the leek and mango mixture. Pour the sauce over the duck slices, garnish with chopped parsley, and serve immediately.

Parma Ham with Fruit

In this classic Italian dish, the slightly salty flavour of air-cured Parma ham provides a marvellous contrast to the sweet fresh fruit.

NUTRITIONAL INFORMATION

Calories .... 198 Sugars 13g
Protein .... 16g Fat 10g
Carbohydrate ... 13g Saturates 3g

10 mins   10 mins

SERVES 4

INGREDIENTS

1 cantaloupe or charentais melon

4 ripe, fresh figs (optional)

12 wafer-thin slices Parma ham

about 4 tsp olive oil, for drizzling

pepper

sprigs of fresh parsley, to garnish

1 Cut the melon in half lengthways. Using a spoon, scoop out the seeds and discard them. Cut each half into 8 thin wedges. Using a paring knife, cut the rind off each slice.

2 Cut the stems off the figs, if using, but do not peel them. Stand the figs upright with the pointed end upwards. Cut each into quarters without cutting all the way through, so you can open them out into attractive 'flowers'.

3 Arrange 3–4 slices of Parma ham on individual serving plates and top with the melon slices and fig 'flowers', if using. Alternatively, arrange the melon slices on the plates and completely cover with the Parma ham; add the figs, if using.

4 Drizzle with olive oil, then grind a little pepper over the top. Garnish with parsley and serve at once.

COOK'S TIP

For an attractive presentation, you can also prepare all the ingredients on one large serving platter and let guests help themselves.

Ham & Pineapple Kebabs

This traditional and much-loved combination of flavours always works well on the barbecue.

NUTRITIONAL INFORMATION

Calories 426   Sugars 11g
Protein .... 31g   Fat 29g
Carbohydrate .... 11g   Saturates 13g

🧀 🧀

🔥 15 mins   🕐 8 mins

SERVES 4

I N G R E D I E N T S

450 g/1 lb thick ham steak

425 g/15 oz canned pineapple pieces in natural juice

225 g/8 oz firm Brie, chilled

2 tbsp sunflower oil

1 garlic clove, crushed

1 tbsp lemon juice

½ tsp ground nutmeg

¼ tsp ground cloves

pepper

sprigs of fresh parsley, to garnish

freshly cooked rice, to serve

1 Cut the ham into even-sized chunks, place in a saucepan of boiling water, and simmer for 5 minutes.

2 Drain the pineapple pieces and reserve 3 tablespoons of the juice. Cut the chilled cheese into large chunks.

3 To make the baste, put the reserved pineapple juice in a small screw-top jar with the oil, garlic, lemon juice, nutmeg and cloves. Add pepper to taste and shake until well combined. Set aside until required.

4 Remove the ham from the pan with a slotted spoon. Thread the ham on to skewers, alternating with the pineapple and cheese pieces.

5 Cook the kebabs over warm coals, turning and basting frequently with the oil and pineapple juice mixture, for 2–4 minutes on each side until the pineapple and ham are hot and the cheese is just beginning to melt. Do not overcook, otherwise the cheese will become runny and the kebabs will become a mess; allow enough time to reheat the ham and for the pineapple to warm through.

6 Remove the kebabs from the heat and serve on a bed of freshly cooked rice, garnished with parsley sprigs.

Ginger Beef with Chilli

Serve these fruity, hot, spicy steaks with noodles. Use a non-stick, ridged grill pan to cook with a minimum of fat.

NUTRITIONAL INFORMATION

Calories 179	Sugars 8g	
Protein 21g	Fat 6g	
Carbohydrate 8g	Saturates 2g	

    40 mins   10 mins

SERVES 4

I N G R E D I E N T S

4 lean beef steaks, such as rump, sirloin or fillet, 100 g/3½ oz each

1 tsp vegetable oil

salt and pepper

strips of fresh red chilli, to garnish

TO SERVE

freshly cooked noodles

2 spring onions, shredded

MARINADE

2 tbsp ginger wine

2.5-cm/1-inch piece of fresh root ginger, finely chopped

1 garlic clove, crushed

1 tsp ground chilli

RELISH

225 g/8 oz fresh pineapple

1 small red pepper

1 fresh red chilli

2 tbsp light soy sauce

1 piece of stem ginger in syrup, drained and chopped

1 Trim any excess fat from the steaks if necessary. Using a meat mallet or covered rolling pin, pound the steaks until they are 1 cm/½ inch thick. Season on both sides with salt and pepper to taste and place in a shallow dish.

2 To make the marinade, combine the ginger wine, fresh root ginger, garlic and ground chilli, then pour it over the meat. Cover with clingfilm and chill for 30 minutes.

3 Meanwhile, make the relish. Peel and finely chop the pineapple and place it in a bowl. Halve, deseed and finely chop the red pepper and chilli. Stir into the pineapple with the soy sauce and stem ginger. Cover with clingfilm and chill until required.

4 Brush a ridged grill pan with the oil and heat until very hot. Drain the beef and add to the pan, pressing down to seal. Lower the heat and cook for 5 minutes. Turn the steaks over and cook for another 5 minutes.

5 Drain the steaks on kitchen paper and transfer to warmed serving plates. Garnish with chilli strips and serve with noodles, spring onions, and the relish.

Summer Puddings

This is a wonderful mixture of summer fruits encased in slices
of white bread, which soak up all the deep-red, flavourful juices.

NUTRITIONAL INFORMATION

Calories	250	Sugars	........41g
Protein	.........4g	Fat	...........4g
Carbohydrate	...53g	Saturates	.......2g

15 mins, plus chilling   5–10 mins

SERVES 6

INGREDIENTS

vegetable oil or butter, for greasing

6–8 thin slices white bread, crusts removed

175 g/6 oz caster sugar

300 ml/10 fl oz water

225 g/8 oz strawberries

450 g/1 lb raspberries

175 g/6 oz blackcurrants and/or
redcurrants

175 g/6 oz blackberries or loganberries

sprigs of fresh mint, to decorate

pouring cream, to serve

1 Grease six 150-ml/5-fl oz moulds with a little butter or oil.

2 Line the moulds with the bread, cutting it so it fits snugly.

3 Place the sugar in a saucepan with the water and heat gently, stirring frequently, until dissolved, then bring to the boil and continue to boil for 2 minutes.

4 Reserve 6 large strawberries for decoration. Add half the raspberries and the rest of the fruits to the syrup in the pan, cutting the strawberries in half if large, and simmer gently for a few minutes until they are beginning to soften but still retain their shape.

5 Spoon the fruits and some of the liquid into the moulds. Cover with more slices of bread. Spoon a little juice around the sides of the moulds so the bread is well soaked. Cover with a saucer, place a heavy weight on top, then leave to cool. Chill thoroughly, preferably overnight.

6 Process the remaining raspberries in a food processor or blender, or press through a non-metallic sieve. Add enough of the liquid from the fruits to give a coating consistency.

7 Turn out the puddings on to serving plates and spoon over the raspberry sauce. Decorate with the mint sprigs and reserved strawberries and serve with cream.

Raspberry Fool

This dish is very easy to make and can be prepared
in advance and stored in the refrigerator until required.

NUTRITIONAL INFORMATION

Calories 288   Sugars 19g
Protein . . . . .4g   Fat 22g
Carbohydrate . . .19g   Saturates 14g

🍧 1¼ hrs   🕐 0 mins

SERVES 4

I N G R E D I E N T S

300 g/10½ oz fresh raspberries

6 tbsp icing sugar

300 ml/10 fl oz crème fraîche or thick
  natural yogurt, plus extra to decorate

½ tsp vanilla extract

2 egg whites

raspberries and lemon balm leaves,
  to decorate

1 Put the raspberries and icing sugar in
a food processor or blender and
process until smooth, or press through a
sieve with the back of a spoon.

2 Reserve 1 tablespoon per portion of
crème fraîche for decorating.

3 Put the remaining crème fraîche and
the vanilla extract in a bowl and stir
in the raspberry mixture.

4 Whisk the egg whites in a separate
mixing bowl until stiff peaks form.
Gently fold the egg whites into the
raspberry mixture using a metal spoon
until fully incorporated.

5 Spoon the raspberry fool into
individual serving dishes and chill for
at least 1 hour. Decorate with the reserved
crème fraîche or yogurt, raspberries and
lemon balm leaves, and serve.

COOK'S TIP

Although this dessert is best
made with fresh raspberries in
season, an acceptable result
can be achieved with frozen
raspberries, which are available
from most food shops.

Mint-chocolate Gelato

Rich, creamy gelati, or ice creams, are one of the great Italian culinary contributions to the world. This version is made with fresh mint.

NUTRITIONAL INFORMATION

Calories 575	Sugars 53g	
Protein 17g	Fat 34g	
Carbohydrate ...54g	Saturates 18g	

5–6 hrs   20 mins

SERVES 4

INGREDIENTS

6 large eggs

150 g/5½ oz caster sugar

300 ml/10 fl oz milk

150 ml/5 fl oz double cream

large handful of fresh mint leaves, rinsed and dried, plus extra to decorate

2 drops green food colouring (optional)

55 g/2 oz plain chocolate, finely chopped

shavings of plain chocolate, to decorate (optional)

1 Put the eggs and sugar in a heatproof bowl that will sit over a saucepan with plenty of room underneath. Using an electric mixer, beat the eggs and sugar together until thick and creamy.

2 Put the milk and cream in the saucepan and bring to a simmer, stirring, until small bubbles appear around the edge. Pour on to the eggs, whisking constantly. Rinse the pan and put 2.5 cm/ 1 inch water in the bottom. Put the bowl on top, making sure the base does not touch the water. Turn the heat to medium–high and cook, stirring, for 1 minute.

3 Transfer the mixture to a saucepan and cook, stirring constantly, until it is thick enough to coat the back of the spoon and leave a mark when you pull your finger across it.

4 Tear the mint leaves and stir them into the custard. Remove the custard from the heat. Leave to cool, then cover and allow to infuse for at least 2 hours, chilling for the last 30 minutes.

5 Strain the mixture through a small nylon sieve to remove the pieces of mint. Stir in the food colouring, if using. Transfer to a freezer container and freeze the mixture for 1–2 hours until frozen 2.5 cm/1 inch from the sides.

6 Scrape into a bowl and beat again until smooth. Stir in the chocolate, smooth the top and cover with clingfilm or foil.

7 Freeze until set, for up to 3 months. Soften in the refrigerator for 20 minutes before serving. Decorate with mint leaves and chocolate shavings.

Melon & Kiwi Salad

This is a refreshing fruit salad, ideal to serve after a rich meal. Galia melon is used here, but Charentais or cantaloupe melons are also good.

NUTRITIONAL INFORMATION

Calories 88	Sugars 17g
Protein 1g	Fat 0.2g
Carbohydrate ...17g	Saturates 0g

🍧 1¼ hrs   🕐 0 mins

SERVES 4

I N G R E D I E N T S

½ galia melon

2 kiwi fruit

18–20 white seedless grapes

1 papaya, halved

3 tbsp orange-flavoured liqueur, such as Cointreau

1 tbsp chopped lemon verbena, lemon balm, or mint

sprigs of lemon verbena, or whole cape gooseberries, to decorate

1 Remove the seeds from the melon, cut it into 4 slices, and carefully cut away the skin. Cut the flesh into cubes and put them into a bowl.

2 Peel the kiwi fruit and cut across into slices. Add to the melon with the white grapes.

3 Remove the seeds from the papaya and cut off the skin. Slice the flesh thickly and cut into diagonal pieces. Add to the fruit bowl and mix well.

4 Mix together the orange-flavoured liqueur and the chopped lemon verbena in a small bowl, pour over the fruit, and leave to macerate for 1 hour, stirring occasionally.

5 Spoon the fruit salad into glasses, pour over the juices, and then decorate with lemon verbena sprigs or cape gooseberries.

COOK'S TIP

Lemon balm or sweet balm is a fragrant, lemon-scented plant with slightly hairy, serrated leaves and a pronounced lemon flavour. Lemon verbena can also be used – this has an even stronger lemon flavour and smooth, elongated leaves.

Balsamic Strawberries

Generations of Italian cooks have known that the unlikely combination of freshly ground black pepper and ripe, juicy strawberries is fantastic.

NUTRITIONAL INFORMATION

Calories 132   Sugars 5g
Protein .... 1g   Fat 12g
Carbohydrate ....5g   Saturates 7g

 4¼ hrs   0 mins

SERVES 4–6

INGREDIENTS

450 g/1 lb fresh strawberries

2–3 tbsp balsamic vinegar

fresh mint leaves, torn, plus extra to decorate (optional)

115–175 g/4–6 oz mascarpone cheese

pepper

1 Wipe the strawberries with a damp cloth, rather than rinsing them, so they do not become soggy. Using a paring knife, cut off the green stalks at the top and use the tip of the knife to remove the core or hull.

COOK'S TIP

This is most enjoyable when it is made with the best-quality balsamic vinegar, one that has aged slowly and has turned thick and syrupy. Unfortunately, the genuine mixture is always expensive. Less expensive versions are artificially sweetened and coloured with caramel.

2 Cut each hulled strawberry in half lengthways or into quarters if large. Transfer to a bowl.

3 Add the balsamic vinegar, allowing ½ tablespoon per person. Add several twists of ground black pepper, then gently stir together. Cover with clingfilm and chill for up to 4 hours.

4 Just before serving, stir in torn fresh mint leaves to taste. Spoon the mascarpone into bowls and spoon the strawberries on top. Decorate with a few mint leaves, if desired. Sprinkle with extra pepper to taste.

Orange & Bitters Sorbet

This smooth, pale-pink sorbet is made from a distinctive Italian drink and freshly squeezed orange juice. It makes a cooling, tangy dessert.

NUTRITIONAL INFORMATION

Calories 212	Sugars 52g
Protein 2g	Fat 0g
Carbohydrate . . .52g	Saturates 0g

 3 hrs   🕐 3–5 mins

SERVES 4–6

I N G R E D I E N T S

3–4 large oranges

225 g/8 oz caster sugar

600 ml/1 pint water

3 tbsp red Italian bitters, such as Campari

2 extra-large egg whites

TO DECORATE

fresh mint leaves

crystallised citrus peel (optional)

1 Working over a bowl to catch any juice, pare the zest from 3 of the oranges, without removing the bitter white pith. If some of the pith does come off with the zest, use the knife to scrape it off. Reserve the zest.

2 Put the caster sugar and water in a saucepan and stir over a low heat until dissolved. Increase the heat and boil for 2 minutes, without stirring. Using a wet pastry brush, brush any crystals down the side of the pan, if necessary.

3 Remove the pan from the heat and pour into a heatproof, non-metallic bowl. Add the reserved orange zest and set aside to steep while the mixture cools to room temperature.

4 Roll the 3 pared oranges back and forth on a work surface, pressing them down firmly. Cut them in half and squeeze 125 ml/4 fl oz of juice from them. If you need more juice, squeeze the remaining orange. When the syrup is cool, stir in the orange juice and bitters. Strain into a container, cover, and chill for at least 30 minutes.

5 Transfer the mixture to a freezerproof container and freeze for 1 hour, then place in a bowl and beat to break up the ice crystals. Put back in the container and freeze for 30 minutes. Repeat twice more, freezing for 30 minutes and whisking each time. Alternatively, put the mixture in an ice-cream maker and churn for about 15 minutes.

6 Whisk the egg whites in a clean, grease-free bowl until stiff peaks form. Add them to the ice cream in a bowl, beat, freeze for 30 minutes, then beat again. Alternatively, add the egg whites to the mixture in the ice-cream maker and continue churning for 5 minutes. Transfer to a shallow, freezerproof container, cover, and freeze for up to 2 months.

7 About 15 minutes before serving, place the ice cream in the refrigerator to soften, then scoop into bowls and serve decorated with mint leaves, and crystallised citrus peel if desired.

Lemon Granita

This iced dessert is soft and granular and has a sharp, zingy flavour, which is refreshing and ideal for rounding off any rich meal.

NUTRITIONAL INFORMATION	
Calories 78	Sugars 20g
Protein 1g	Fat 0g
Carbohydrate . . .20g	Saturates 0g

 4 hrs   🕐 5 mins

SERVES 4–6

I N G R E D I E N T S

4 large unwaxed lemons

100 g/3½ oz caster sugar

700 ml/1¼ pints water

sprigs of fresh mint, to decorate (optional)

scooped-out lemon shells, to serve (optional)

1 Pare 6 strips of rind from 1 of the lemons, then finely grate the remaining rind from the remaining lemons, being very careful not to remove any bitter white pith.

2 Roll the lemons back and forth on a work surface, pressing down firmly. Cut each in half and squeeze 125 ml/4 fl oz juice from them. Add the grated rind to the juice. Set aside.

VARIATION

Lemon-scented herbs add a unique and unexpected flavour. Add 4 small sprigs of lemon balm or 2 sprigs of lemon thyme to the syrup in step 3. Remove and discard with the pared rind in step 4. Or stir ½ tablespoon finely chopped lemon thyme into the mixture in step 4.

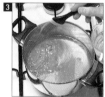  

3 Put the pared strips of lemon rind, sugar and water in a saucepan and stir over a low heat to dissolve the sugar. Increase the heat and boil for 4 minutes, without stirring. Use a wet pastry brush to brush down any spatters on the side of the pan. Turn off the heat and stir in the lemon juice, then pour into a heatproof, non-metallic bowl, and cool.

4 Remove the strips of rind from the syrup. Stir in the grated rind. Transfer to a shallow metal container, cover, and freeze for up to 3 months.

5 Chill serving bowls 30 minutes before serving. To serve, invert the container on to a chopping board. Rinse a clean cloth in very hot water, wring it out, then rub it on the bottom of the container for 15 seconds. Give the container a shake and the mixture should fall out.

6 Break up the granita with a knife and then transfer to a food processor. Process until it becomes granular. Serve in the chilled bowls (or in scooped-out lemons), decorated with sprigs of fresh mint if using.